Wood

MW01233873

Smoker and Grill

Cookbook

A Beginner's Guide To Discover Delicious, Healthy

and Simple Wood Pellet Grill Recipes for

Everyday

Trevor Foster

Disclaimer Notice:

Please note the information contained within this document is for educational and entertainment purposes only. All effort has been executed to present accurate, up to date, and reliable, complete information. No warranties of any kind are declared or implied. Readers acknowledge that the author is not engaging in the rendering of legal, financial, medical or professional advice. The content within this book has been derived from various sources. Please consult a licensed professional before attempting any techniques outlined in this book.

By reading this document, the reader agrees that under no circumstances is the author responsible for any losses, direct or indirect, which are incurred as a result of the use of information contained within this document, including, but not limited to, errors, omissions, or inaccuracies.

Table of Content

Introduction

Thank you for purchasing **Wood Pellet Smoker and Grill Cookbook: A Beginner's Guide To Discover Delicious, Healthy and Simple Wood Pellet Grill Recipes for Everyday**

A religion that has real rituals that every true American must know: we are referring to the barbecue, the bbq, and the strong culture and tradition that transforms a dish into a ritual. Barbecue is the expression of the quintessence of America, the quintessence of Sunday rituals and open air barbecue is the expression of the quintessence of America, the quintessence that can be found in front of a smoking grill. There are two main events: Independence Day (July 4) and the Super Bowl. But the ritual continues in the backyard on Sundays or during summer weekends. Not just one custom, but several traditions that change from state to state. Underlying it is an absolute theory: low & slow, cooking is slow and prolonged.

Chicken & Beef Recipes

Chinese BBQ Pork

Preparation Time: 10 minutes

Cooking Time: 20 minutes

Servings: 6

Ingredients:

Pork & Marinade

- 2 Pork Tenderloins, Silver Skin Removed
- ¼ Cup Hoisin Sauce
- ¼ Cup Honey
- 1 ½ tbsp. Brown sugar
- 3 tbsp. Soy Sauce
- 1 tbsp. Asian Sesame Oil
- 1 tbsp. Oyster Sauce, Optional
- 1 tsp. Chinese Five Spice
- 1 Garlic Clove, Minced
- 2 tsp. Red Food Coloring, Optional

Five Spice Dipping Sauce

- ¼ Cup Ketchup
- 3 tbsp. Brown sugar
- 1 tsp Yellow Mustard

- ¼ tsp Chinese Five Spice

Directions:

1.   In a medium bowl, whisk together marinade thoroughly, making sure brown Sugar: is dissolved. Add pork and marinade to a glass pan or resealable plastic bag and marinate for at least 8 hours or overnight, occasionally turning to ensure all pork sides are well coated.

2.   When ready to cook, set the temperature to 225°F and preheat, lid closed for 15 minutes.

3.   Remove pork from marinade and boil marinade in a saucepan over medium-high heat on the stovetop for 3 minutes to use for basting pork. Cool slightly, then whisk in 2 additional tbsp. of honey.

4.   Arrange the tenderloins on the grill grate and smoke pork until the internal temperature reaches 145°F.

5.   Baste pork with reserved marinade halfway through cooking. Remove pork from grill and, if desired, increase the temperature to High and return pork to grill for a few minutes per side to slight char and set the sauce. Alternatively, you can broil in the oven, just a couple of minutes per side.

6.   For the 5 Spice Sauce: In a small saucepan over low heat, mix ketchup, brown sugar, mustard, and five-spice until Sugar: is dissolved and sauce is smooth. Let cool, and serve chilled or at room temperature.

7.   Serve pork immediately with Jasmine rice, or cool and refrigerate for future use as an appetizer, served with Five Spice dipping sauce and toasted sesame seeds. Enjoy!

8.   In a medium bowl, whisk together marinade thoroughly, making sure brown Sugar: is dissolved. Add pork and marinade to a glass pan or resealable plastic bag and marinate for at least 8 hours or overnight, occasionally turning to ensure all sides of pork are well coated.

9.   When ready to cook, set the temperature to 225°F and preheat, lid closed for 15 minutes.

10.   Remove pork from marinade and boil marinade in a saucepan over medium-high heat on the stovetop for 3 minutes to use for basting pork. Cool slightly, then whisk in 2 additional tbsp. of honey.

11.   Arrange the tenderloins on the grill grate and smoke pork until the internal temperature reaches 145°F.

12.　　Baste pork with reserved marinade halfway through cooking. Remove pork from grill and, if desired, increase the temperature to High and return pork to grill for a few minutes per side to slight char and set the sauce. Alternatively, you can broil in the oven, just a couple of minutes per side.

13.　　For the 5 Spice Sauce: In a small saucepan over low heat, mix ketchup, brown sugar, mustard, and five-spice until Sugar: is dissolved and sauce is smooth. Let cool, and serve chilled or at room temperature.

14.　　Serve pork immediately with Jasmine rice, or cool and refrigerate for future use as an appetizer, served with Five Spice dipping sauce and toasted sesame seeds. Enjoy!

Nutrition:

- Calories: 324

- Fat: 11.6g

- Cholesterol: 6mg

- Sodium: 1029mg

Grilled Chicken Kebabs

Preparation Time: 10 minutes

Cooking Time: 40 minutes

Servings: 8

Ingredients:

For Marinade

- ½ cup Olive oil

- 1 tbsp. lemon, juiced

- 2 tbsp. White vinegar

- 1 ½ tbsp. Salt

- 1 tbsp. Minced garlic

- 1 ½ tbsp. Fresh thyme

- 2 tbsp. Fresh Italian parsley

- 2 tbsp. Fresh chives

- ½ tbsp. Ground pepper

For Kebabs

- Orange, yellow, and red bell peppers

- 1 ½ Chicken breasts, boneless and skinless

- 10–12 medium-sized mushrooms of your choice

Directions:

1.   Mix all the ingredients for the marinade.

2.   Add the chicken and mushrooms to the marinade and put them in the refrigerator.

3.   Preheat your traeger grill to 450°F.

4.   Remove the marinated chicken from the refrigerator and place it on the grill.

5.   Grill the kebabs on one side for 6 minutes. Flip to grill on the other side.

6.   Serve with a side dish of your choice.

Nutrition:

• Carbs: 1 g

• Fat: 2 g

• Sodium: 582 mg

Rub-Injected Pork Shoulder

Preparation Time: 15 minute

Cooking Time: 16 to 20 hours

Servings: 8 to 12

Ingredients:

- 1 (6 to 8-pound) bone-in pork shoulder

- 2 cups Tea Injectable made with Not-Just-for-Pork Rub

- 2 tbsp. yellow mustard

- 1 batch Not-Just-for-Pork Rub

Directions:

1. Supply your smoker with a traeger and follow the manufacturer's specific start-up procedure. Preheat the grill, with the lid closed, to 225°F.

2. Inject the pork shoulder throughout with the tea injectable.

3. Coat the pork shoulder all over with mustard and season it with the rub. Using your hands, work the rub into the meat.

4.   Place the shoulder directly on the grill grate and smoke until its internal temperature reaches 160°F and a dark bark has formed on the exterior.

5.   Pull the shoulder from the grill and wrap it completely in aluminum foil or butcher paper.

6.   Increase the grill's temperature to 350°F.

7.   Return the pork shoulder to the grill and cook until its internal temperature reaches 195°F.

8.   Pull the shoulder from the grill and place it in a cooler. Cover the cooler and let the pork rest for 1 or 2 hours.

9.   Remove the pork shoulder from the cooler and unwrap it. Remove the shoulder bone and pull the pork apart using just your fingers. Serve immediately.

Nutrition:

•   Calories: 688

•   Protein: 58.9g

•   Carbs: 2.7g

•   Fat: 47.3g

Reverse Seared Flank Steak

Preparation Time: 10 minutes

Cooking Time: 10 minutes

Servings: 2

Ingredients:

- 1.5 lb. Flanks steak
- 1 tbsp. salt
- ½ onion powder
- ¼ tbsp. garlic powder
- ½ black pepper, coarsely ground

Directions:

1. Preheat your traeger grill to 225°F.

2. In a mixing bowl, mix salt, onion powder, garlic powder, and pepper. Generously rub the steak with the mixture.

3. Place the steaks on the preheated grill, close the lid, and let the steak cook.

4. Crank up the grill to high then let it heat. The steak should be off the grill and tented with foil to keep it warm.

5.   Once the grill is heated up to 450°F, place the steak

back and grill for 3 minutes per side.

6.   Remove from heat, pat with butter, and serve. Enjoy.

Nutrition:

- Calories: 112, Fat: 5g,

- Protein: 16g, Sugar: 0g,

- Fiber: 0g, Sodium: 737mg

Smoked Spare Ribs

Preparation Time: 25 minutes

Cooking Time: 4 to 6 hours Servings: 4 to 8

Ingredients:

- 2 (2 or 3-pound) racks spare ribs

- 2 tbsp. yellow mustard

- 1 batch Sweet Brown Sugar Rub

- ¼ cup Bill's Best BBQ Sauce

Directions:

1.   Supply your smoker with traeger and follow the manufacturer's specific start-up procedure. Preheat the grill, with the lid closed, to 225°F.

2.   Remove the membrane from the backside of the ribs. This can be done by cutting just through the membrane in an X pattern and working a paper towel between the membrane and the ribs to pull it off.Coat the ribs on both sides with mustard and season with the rub. Using your hands, work the rub into the meat.Place the ribs directly on the grill grate and smoke until their internal temperature reaches between 190°F and 200°F.Baste both sides of the ribs with barbecue

sauce.Increase the grill's temperature to 300°F and continue to cook the ribs for 15 minutes more.

3.   Remove the racks from the grill, cut them into individual ribs, and serve immediately.

Nutrition: Calories: 277 Fat: 23g Protein: 16g

Simple Pork Tenderloin

Preparation Time: 15min

Cooking Time: 20min

Servings: 4 - 6

Ingredients:

*   2 Pork Tenderloins (12–15 oz. each)

*   6 tbsp. hot Sauce, Louisiana style

*   6 tbsp. melted butter

*   Cajun seasoning as needed

Directions:

1. Trim the silver skin from the meat.

2. In a large bowl, combine the hot sauce and melted butter. Roll the meat in this mixture and season with Cajun seasoning.

3. Preheat the grill to 400°F with the lid closed.

4. Grill the meat for 8 minutes on each side. The internal temperature should be 145°F and if you want well-done, cook until 160°F.

5. Let it rest for a few minutes before cutting. Serve with your favorite side dish and enjoy!

Nutrition

- Calories: 150

- Protein: 20g

- Carbs: 0

- Fat: 3g

Ground Turkey Burgers

Preparation Time: 15 minutes

Cooking Time: 50 minutes

Servings: 6

Ingredients:

- 2/3 cup bread crumbs.

- ½ cup chopped celery

- ¼ cup chopped onion

- 1 tbsp. minced parsley

- 1 tsp. Worcestershire sauce

- 1 tsp. dried oregano

- ½ tsp. salt to taste

- ¼ tsp. pepper

- 1-¼ pounds lean ground turkey

- 6 hamburger buns

- Optional topping

- 1 sliced tomato

- 1 sliced onion

- Lettuce leaves

- Beaten egg

Directions:

1.   Using a small mixing bowl, add in all the ingredients on the list aside from the turkey and buns then mix properly to combine.

2.   Add in the ground turkey then mix everything to combine. Feel free to use clean hands for this. Make about six patties of the mixture then set aside.

3.   Preheat your Traeger Smoker and Grill to 375°F, place the turkey patties on the grill and grill for about forty-five minutes until its internal temperature reads 165°F. to assemble, use a knife to split the bun into two, top with the prepared burger and your favorite topping then close with another half of the buns, serve.

Nutrition:

• Calories: 293

• Fat: 11g

• Carbohydrate: 27g

• Fiber: 4g

• Protein: 22g

Smoked Chicken Leg Quarter in a Traeger Grill

Preparation Time: 10 minutes

Cooking Time: 30 minutes

Servings: 8

Ingredients:

- 4 Chicken leg quarters

- 3 tbsp. dry rub spice mix for chicken

- 1 tbsp. olive oil

- Salt

Directions:

1. Wash and dry the chicken legs.

2. Add some olive oil. Sprinkle the dry rub spice mix all over the chicken.

3. Set aside for 20 minutes.

4. Preheat the grill on 'smoke' for 10–15 minutes.

5. Place the chicken on the grill with skin side up to smoke for 1 hour.

6. Increase the heat to 350°F and cook for another 30 to 60 minutes, depending on the size of the pieces and the number of chicken legs.

7. Poke into the thickest part of the thighs.

8. When done, serve one leg quarter with a side sauce of your choice.

Nutrition: Carbs: 1.5 g Protein: 16 g Fat: 21 g

Bacon-Wrapped Pork Tenderloin

Preparation Time: 15 minutes

Cooking Time: 40 minutes

Servings: 4

Ingredients:

- 1 pork tenderloin.

- 4 strips of bacon.

Rub:

- 8 tbsp. brown sugar.

- 3 tbsp. kosher salt to taste.

- 1 tbsp. chili powder.

- 1 tsp. black pepper to taste.

- 1 tsp. onion powder.

- 1 tsp. garlic powder.

Directions:

1. Using a small mixing bowl, add sugar, chili powder, onion powder, garlic powder, salt, and pepper to taste, mix properly to combine, and set aside. Use a sharp knife to trim off fats present on the pork, then coat with ¼ of the prepared rub. Make sure you coat all sides.

2.   Roll each pork tenderloin with a piece of bacon, lay the meat on a cutting board, then pound with a meat mallet to give an even thickness, secure the ends of the bacon with toothpicks to hold still. Coat the meat again with just a little more of the rub spice, then set aside.

3.   Preheat a Traeger smoker and Grill to 350°F, place the pork tenderloin on the grill, and grill for about fifteen minutes. Increase the temperature of the grill to 400°F and cook for another fifteen minutes until it is cooked through and reads an internal temperature of 145°F.

4.   Once cooked, let the pork rest for a few minutes, slice, and serve.

Nutrition:

- Calories: 236

- Fat 8g

- Carbs: 10g

- Protein: 29g

Smoke Roasted Chicken

Preparation Time: 20 minutes

Cooking Time: 1 hour 20 minutes

Servings: 4–6

Ingredients:

• 8 tbsp. butter, room temperature

• 1 clove garlic, minced

• 1 scallion, minced

• 2 tbsp. fresh herbs such as thyme, rosemary, sage or parsley

• Chicken rub, as needed

• Lemon juice

• As needed vegetable oil

Directions:

1. In a small cooking bowl, mix the scallions, garlic, butter, minced fresh herbs, 1–½ tsp. of the rub, and lemon juice. Mix with a spoon.

2. Remove any giblets from the cavity of the chicken. Wash the chicken inside and out with cold running water. Dry thoroughly with paper towels.

3.   Sprinkle a generous amount of Chicken Rub inside the cavity of the chicken.

4.   Gently loosen the skin around the chicken breast and slide in a few tbsp. of the herb butter under the skin and cover.

5.   Cover the outside with the remaining herb butter.

6.   Insert the chicken wings behind the back. Tie both legs together with a butcher's string.

7.   Powder the outside of the chicken with more Chicken Rub then insert sprigs of fresh herbs inside the cavity of the chicken.

8.   Set temperature to High and preheat, lid closed for 15 minutes.

9.   Oil the grill with vegetable oil. Move the chicken on the grill grate, breast-side up then close the lid.

10.   After the chicken has cooked for 1 hour, lift the lid. If chicken is browning too quickly, cover the breast and legs with aluminum foil.

11.   Close the lid then continue to roast the chicken until an instant-read meat thermometer inserted into the thickest part registers a temperature of 165°F

12.   Take off the chicken from the grill and let rest for 5 minutes. Serve, Enjoy!

Nutrition:

- Calories: 222 Carbs: 11g

- Protein: 29g

- Fat: 4g

- Cholesterol: 62mg

- Sodium: 616mg

- Potassium 620mg

Carolina Pork Ribs

Preparation Time: 12 Hours

Cooking Time: 3 Hours

Servings: 6

Ingredients:

- 2 racks pork spareribs

- ½ cup "Burning' Love" Rub

- 1 cup Carolina Basting Sauce

- 1 cup Carolina BBQ Sauce

Directions:

1. Prepare ribs by removing the membrane from the underside. Trim off any loose fat, and season ribs with rub, wrap in plastic wrap and refrigerate overnight.

2. Allow ribs to warm for 1 hour. Preheat traeger grill to 280°F.

3. If you want to sauce the ribs, do so 5 minutes before they're done, turning every minute, and observe.

Nutrition:

- Calories: 290

- Carbs: 5g

- Fat: 23g

- Protein: 15g

Traeger Grilled Chicken

Preparation Time: 10 minutes

Cooking Time: 1 hour 30 minutes

Servings: 6

Ingredients:

- 5 lb. whole chicken

- ½ cup oil

- Traeger chicken rub

Directions:

1. Preheat the Traeger on the smoke setting with the lid open for 5 minutes. Close the lid and let it heat for 15 minutes or until it reaches 450°F.

2. Use baker's twine to tie the chicken legs together then rub it with oil. Coat the chicken with the rub and place it on the grill.

3. Grill for 70 minutes with the lid closed or until it reaches an internal temperature of 165°F.

4. Remove the chicken from the Traeger and let rest for 15 minutes. Cut and serve.

Nutrition:

- Calories: 935

- Fat: 53g

- Protein: 107g

- Fiber: 0g

- Sodium: 320mg

Homemade Turkey Gravy

Preparation Time: 20 minutes

Cooking Time: 3 hours 20 minutes

Servings: 8-12

Ingredients:

- 1 turkey, neck

- 2 large Onion, eight

- 4 celeries, stalks

- 4 large carrots, fresh

- 8 clove garlic, smashed

- 8 thyme sprigs

- 4 cup chicken broth

- 1 tsp. chicken broth

- 1 tsp. salt

- 1 tsp. cracked black pepper

- 1 butter, sticks

- 1 cup all-purpose flour

Directions:

1.   When ready to cook, set the temperature to 350°F and preheat the traeger grill with the lid closed, for 15 minutes.

2.   Place turkey neck, celery, carrot (roughly chopped), garlic, onion, and thyme on a roasting pan. Add four cups of chicken stock then season with salt and pepper.

3.   Move the prepped turkey on the rack into the roasting pan and place in the traeger grill.

4.   Cook for about 3–4 hours until the breast reaches 160°F. The turkey will continue to cook and it will reach a finished internal temperature of 165°F.

5.   Strain the drippings into a saucepan and simmer on low.

6.   In a saucepan, mix butter (cut into 8 pieces) and flour with a whisk stirring until golden tan. This takes about 8 minutes, stirrings constantly.

7.   Whisk the drippings into the roux then cook until it comes to a boil. Season with salt and pepper.

Nutrition:

•   Calories: 160

•   Carbohydrate 27g

- Protein: 55g

- Fat 23g

- Saturated Fat: 6.1g

Pork Collar with Rosemary Marinade

Preparation Time: 15 minutes Cooking Time: 30 minutes

Servings: 6   Ingredients:

- 1 Pork Collar (3–4lb.)
- 3 tbsp. Rosemary, fresh
- 3 minced Shallots
- 2 tbsp. chopped Garlic
- ½ cup Bourbon
- 2 tsp. Coriander, ground
- 1 bottle Apple Ale
- 1 tsp. ground Black pepper
- 2 tsp. Salt
- 3 tbsp. oil

Directions:

1.   In a Ziploc bag, combine the black pepper, salt, canola oil, apple ale, bourbon, coriander, garlic, shallots, and rosemary.

2.   Cut the meat into slabs (2 inches) and marinate in the refrigerator overnight.

3.   Preheat the grill to 450°F with the lid closed. Grill the meat for 5 minutes and lower the temperature to 325°F. Pour the marinade over the meat. Cook 25 minutes more.

4.   Cook until the internal temperature of the meat is 160°F.

5.   Serve and enjoy!

Nutrition: Calories: 420 Protein: 30g Carbs: 4g Fat: 26g

Typical Nachos

Preparation Time: 15 minutes

Cooking Time: 10 minutes

Servings: 4

Ingredients:

- 2 cups leftover smoked pulled pork

- 1 small sweet onion, diced

- 1 medium tomato, diced

- 1 jalapeño pepper, seeded and diced

- 1 garlic clove, minced

- 1 tsp. salt

- 1 tsp. freshly ground black pepper

- 1 bag tortilla chips

- 1 cup shredded Cheddar cheese

- ½ cup Bill's Best BBQ Sauce, divided

- ½ cup shredded jalapeño Monterey Jack cheese

- ½ lime, juiced

- 1 avocado, halved, pitted, and sliced

- 2 tbsp. sour cream

- 1 tbsp. chopped fresh cilantro

Directions:

1.   Supply your smoker with traeger and follow the manufacturer's specific start-up procedure. Preheat, with the lid, closed, to 375°F.

2.   Heat the pulled pork in the microwave.

3.   In a medium bowl, combine the onion, tomato, jalapeño, garlic, salt, and pepper, and set aside.

4.   Arrange half of the tortilla chips in a large cast-iron skillet. Spread half of the warmed pork on top and cover with the Cheddar cheese. Top with half of the onion-jalapeño mixture, then drizzle with ¼ cup of barbecue sauce

5.   Layer on the remaining tortilla chips, then the remaining pork and the Monterey Jack cheese. Top with the remaining onion-jalapeño mixture and drizzle with the remaining ¼ cup of barbecue sauce.

6.   Place the skillet on the grill, close the lid, and smoke for about 10 minutes, or until the cheese is melted and bubbly. (Watch to make sure your chips don't burn!)

7.   Squeeze the lime juice over the nachos, top with the avocado slices and sour cream, and garnish with the cilantro before serving hot.

Nutrition:

- Calories: 688

- Protein: 58.9g

- Carbs: 2.7g

- Fat: 47.3g

- Sugar: 0.2g

Traeger Chicken Breast

Preparation Time: 10 minutes

Cooking Time: 15 minutes

Servings: 6

Ingredients:

- 3 chicken breasts

- 1 tbsp. avocado oil

- ¼ tbsp. garlic powder

- ¼ tbsp. onion powder

- ¾ tbsp. salt

- ¼ tbsp. pepper

Directions:

1. Preheat your Traeger to 375°F

2. Cut the chicken breast into halves lengthwise then coat with avocado oil.

3. Season with garlic powder, onion powder, salt, and pepper.

4. Place the chicken on the grill and cook for 7 minutes on each side or until the internal temperature reaches 165°F

Nutrition:

- Calories: 120

- Fat: 4g

- Protein: 19g

- Fiber: 0g

- Sodium: 309mg

Slow Smoked Pork Belly Sliders

Preparation Time: 20 minutes

Cooking Time: 4 hours

Servings: 8 to 10

Ingredients:

- 4–5 lbs. pork belly, cut into 1-inch chunks

- 1–2 cups cabbage slaw

- 12 brioche slider

- 2 cups cherry cola

- 1 tsp coriander

- ½ cup dark brown Sugar:

- 1 tsp onion powder

- 1 cup ketchup

- 1 tsp liquid smoke

- 1 tsp garlic powder

- ½ cup molasses

- 1 tbsp. Worcestershire sauce

- 1 tsp. ground ginger

- Sweet heat rub & grill

- Salt and pepper

- 1 tsp. smoked paprika

Directions:

For the BBQ sauce

1.   Take a saucepan and add ketchup along with molasses, liquid smoke, dark brown sugar, onion powder, coriander, ground ginger, cherry cola, garlic powder, Worcestershire sauce, smoked paprika, and salt-pepper

2.   Cook it on medium heat till everything seem to have combined well and begins to bubble

3.   Reduce the heat to slow and let the sauce thicken till it simmers properly and keep aside.

For the main course

1.   Preheat the grill to 225°F

2.   Now cut the surface of the pork belly using a sharp knife and make ¼ inch deep marks

3.   Apply sweet heat rub generously on all parts of the pork belly, and then let it sit at room temperature for 20 minutes

4.   Place it on the grill and smoke it for nearly 4 hours

5.   In between, brush it with BBQ sauce every 30 minutes

6. Remove it from the smoker and cut into small bite-sized portions

7. Place it on the brioche buns and top it with BBQ sauce and coleslaw

8. Serve

Nutrition:

- Calories: 310

- Fats: 26g

- Protein: 17g

Grilled Asian Chicken Burgers

Preparation Time: 5 minutes

Cooking Time: 50 minutes

Servings: 4-6

Ingredients:

- Pound chicken, ground

- 1 cup panko breadcrumbs

- 1 cup parmcsan cheese

- 1 small jalapeno, diced

- 2 whole scallions, minced

- 2 garlic clove

- ¼ cup minced cilantro leaves

- 2 tbsp. mayonnaise

- 2 tbsp. chili sauce

- 1 tbsp. soy sauce

- 1 tbsp. ginger, minced

- 2 tsp. lemon juice

- 2 tsp. lemon zest

- 1 tsp. salt

- 1 tsp. ground black pepper

- 8 hamburger buns

- 1 tomato, sliced

- Arugula, fresh

- 1 red onion sliced

Directions:

1. Align a rimmed baking sheet with aluminum foil then spray with nonstick cooking spray.

2. In a large bowl, combine the chicken, jalapeno, scallion, garlic, cilantro, panko, Parmesan, chili sauce, soy sauce ginger, mayonnaise, lemon juice and zest, and salt and pepper.

3. Work the mixture with your fingers until the ingredients are well combined. If the mixture looks too wet to form patties and add additional more panko.

4. Wash your hands under cold running water, form the meat into 8 patties, each about an inch larger than the buns and about ¾" thick. Use your thumbs or a tbsp., make a wide, shallow depression in the top of each

5.   Put them on the prepared baking sheet. Spray the tops with nonstick cooking spray. If not cooking right away, cover with plastic wrap and refrigerate.

6.   Set the traeger grill to 350°F then preheat for 15 minutes, lid closed.

7.   Order the burgers, depression-side down, on the grill grate. Remove and discard the foil on the baking sheet so you'll have an uncontaminated surface to transfer the slider when cooked.

8.   Grill the burgers for about 25 to 30 minutes, turning once, or until they release easily from the grill grate when a clean metal spatula is slipped under them. The internal temperature when read on an instant-read meat thermometer should be 160°F.

9.   Spread mayonnaise and arrange a tomato slice, if desired, and a few arugula leaves on one-half of each bun. Top with a grilled burger and red onions, if using, then replace the top half of the bun. Serve immediately. Enjoy

Nutrition:

•   Calories: 329

- Carbs: 10g

- Protein: 21g

- Fat: 23g

Traeger Elk Jerky

Preparation Time: 10 minutes

Cooking Time: 6 hours

Servings: 10

Ingredients:

- 4 Pounds elk hamburger

- ¼ cup soy sauce

- ¼ cup Teriyaki sauce

- ¼ cup Worcestershire sauce

- 1 tbsp. paprika

- 1 tbsp. chili powder

- 1 tbsp. crushed red pepper

- 3 tbsp. hot sauce

- 1 tbsp. pepper

- 1 tbsp. garlic powder

- 1 tbsp. onion salt

- 1 tbsp. salt

Directions:

1. Start by mixing all of the ingredients of the seasoning and the elk hamburger in a large bowl; then let sit in the refrigerator for about 12 hours

2. Light your Traeger smoker to a low temperature of about 160°F

3. Take the elk meat out of your refrigerator and start making strips of the meat manually or with a rolling pin

4. Add smoker wood chips to your Traeger smoker grill and rub some quantity of olive oil over the smoker grate lay out the strips in one row

5. Warm a dehydrator up about halfway during the smoking process

6. Remove the elk jerky meat off your smoker at about 3 hours

7. Line it into the kitchen.

8. Line your dehydrator with the elk jerky meat and keep it in for about 5 to 6 additional hours

9. Serve and enjoy!

Nutrition:

- Calories: 70

- Fat: 1g

- Carbs: 3g

- Fiber: 0g

- Protein: 10g

Delicious BLT Sandwich

Preparation Time: 15 minutes Cooking Time: 35 minutes

Servings: 4-6 Ingredients:

- 8 slices bacon

- ½ romaine heart

- 1sliced tomato

- 4 slices sandwich bread

- 3 tbsp. mayonnaise

- Salted butter

- Sea salt to taste

- Pepper to taste

Directions:

1.   Preheat a Traeger Smoker and Grill to 350°F for about fifteen minutes with its lid closed.

2.   Place the bacon slices on the preheated grill and cook for about fifteen to twenty minutes until they become crispy.

3.   Next, butter both sides of the bread, place a grill pan on the griddle of the Traeger, and toast the bread for a few minutes until they become brown on both sides, set aside.

4.   Using a small mixing bowl, add in the sliced tomatoes, season with salt and pepper to taste then mix to coat.

5.   Next, spread mayo on both sides of the toasted bread, top with the lettuce, tomato, and bacon then enjoy.

Nutrition: Calories: 284 Protein: 19g Fat: 19g Carbs: 11g Fiber: 2g

Turkey with Apricot Barbecue Glaze

Preparation Time: 30 minutes

Cooking Time: 30 minutes

Servings: 4

Ingredients:

*   4 turkey breast fillets

*   4 tbsp. chicken rub

*   1 cup apricot barbecue sauce

Directions:

1. Preheat the Traeger grill to 365°F for 15 minutes while the lid is closed.

2. Season the turkey fillets with the chicken run.

3. Grill the turkey fillets for 5 minutes per side.

4. Brush both sides with the barbecue sauce and grill for another 5 minutes per side.

Serving suggestion: Serve with buttered cauliflower.

Preparation / Cooking Tips: You can sprinkle turkey with chili powder if you want your dish spicy.

Nutrition:

*   Calories: 316

- Fat: 12.3 g

- Carbs: 0 g

- Protein: 29.8 g

- Fiber: 0 g

Traeger Smoked Beef Jerky

Preparation Time: 15 minutes

Cooking Time: 5 hours

Servings: 10

Ingredients:

- 3 lb. sirloin steaks, sliced into ¼ inch thickness

- 2 cups soy sauce

- ½ cup brown Sugar:

- 1 cup pineapple juice

- 2 tbsp. sriracha

- 2 tbsp. red pepper flake

- 2 tbsp. hoisin

- 2 tbsp. onion powder

- 2 tbsp. rice wine vinegar

- 2 tbsp. garlic, minced

Directions:

1.   Mix all the ingredients in a Ziploc bag. Seal the bag and mix until the beef is well coated. Ensure you get as much air as possible from the Ziploc bag.

2.	Put the bag in the fridge overnight to let marinate. Remove the bag from the fridge 1 hour prior to cooking.

3.	Startup your wood pallet grill and set it to smoke setting. Layout the meat on the grill with a half-inch space between them.

4.	Let them cook for 5 hours while turning after every 2–½ hours.

5.	Transfer from the grill and let cool for 30 minutes before serving.

Nutrition:

- Calories: 80,

- Fat: 1g,

- Protein: 14g,

- Sugar: 5g,

- Fiber: 0g,

- Sodium: 650mg

Sweet Sriracha Barbecue Chicken

Preparation Time: 30 minutes

Cooking Time: 1 and ½–2 hours

Servings: 5

Ingredients:

- 1cup sriracha

- ½ cup butter

- ½ cup molasses

- ½ cup ketchup

- ¼ cup firmly packed brown sugar:

- 1 tsp. salt

- 1 tsp. fresh ground black pepper

- 1 whole chicken, cut into pieces

- ½ tsp. fresh parsley leaves, chopped

Directions:

1.   Preheat your smoker to 250°F using cherry wood

2.   Take a medium saucepan and place it over low heat, stir in butter, sriracha, ketchup, molasses, brown sugar, mustard, pepper and salt and keep stirring until the Sugar: and salt dissolves

3.   Divide the sauce into two portions

4.   Brush the chicken half with the sauce and reserve the remaining for serving

5.   Make sure to keep the sauce for serving on the side, and keep the other portion for basting

6.   Transfer chicken to your smoker rack and smoke for about 1 and a half to 2 hours until the internal temperature reaches 165°Fahrenheit

7.   Sprinkle chicken with parsley and serve with reserved Barbecue sauce

Nutrition:

- Calories: 148

- Fats: 0.6g

- Carbs: 10g

- Fiber: 1g

Vegetables and Vegetarian Recipes

Baked Heirloom Tomato Tart

Preparation Time: 20 minutes

Cooking Time: 1 hour and 40 minutes

Servings: 6

Ingredients:

- 1 Sheet Puff Pastry

- 2 Lbs. Heirloom Tomatoes, Various Shapes, and Sizes

- ½ cup Ricotta

- 5 Eggs

- ½ tbsp. Kosher Salt

- ½ tsp. Thyme Leaves

- ½ tsp. Red Pepper Flakes

- Pinch Black Pepper

- 4 Sprigs Thyme

- Salt and Pepper, To Taste

Directions:

1. When ready to cook, set temperature to 350°F and preheat, lid closed for 15 minutes.

2.   Place the puff pastry on a parchment-lined sheet tray, and make a cut ¾ of the way through the pastry, ½" from the edge.

3.   Slice the tomatoes and season with salt. Place on a sheet tray lined with paper towels.

4.   In a small bowl combine the ricotta, 4 of the eggs, salt, thyme leaves, red pepper flakes, and black pepper. Whisk together until combined. Spread the ricotta mixture over the puff pastry, staying within ½" from the edge.

5.   Lay the tomatoes out on top of the ricotta, and sprinkle with salt, pepper, and thyme sprigs.

6.   In a small bowl whisk the last egg. Brush the egg wash onto the exposed edges of the pastry.

7.   Place the sheet tray directly on the grill grate and bake for 45 minutes, rotating half-way through.

8.   When the edges are browned and the moisture from the tomatoes has evaporated, remove from the grill and let cool 5-7 minutes before serving. Enjoy!

Nutrition:

•   Calories: 443

- Protein: 13.8g

- Carbs: 36.3g

Baked Asparagus Pancetta Cheese Tart

Preparation Time: 10 minutes

Cooking Time: 20 to 30 minutes

Servings: 5

Ingredients:

- 1 Sheet Puff Pastry

- 8 Oz Asparagus, Pencil Spears

- 8 Oz Pancetta, Cooked and Drained

- 1 cup Cream

- 4 Eggs

- ¼ cup Goat Cheese

- 4 tbsp. Grated Parmesan

- 1 tbsp. Chopped Chives

- Black Pepper

Directions:

1. When ready to cook, set the temperature to 375°F and preheat, lid closed for 15 minutes.

2. Place the puff pastry on a half sheet tray and score around the perimeter 1-inch in from the edges making sure not

to cut all the way through. Prick the center of the puff pastry with a fork.

3.   Place the sheet tray directly on the grill grate and bake for 15-20 minutes until the pastry has puffed and browned a little bit.

4.   While the pastry bakes combine the cream, 3 eggs, both kinds of cheese, and chives in a small bowl. Whisk to mix well.

5.   Remove the sheet tray from the grill and pour the egg mixture into the puff pastry. Lay the asparagus spears on top of the egg mixture and sprinkle with cooked pancetta.

6.   Whisk the remaining egg in a small bowl and brush the top of the pastry with the egg wash.

7.   Place back on the grill grate and cook for another 15-20 minutes until the egg mixture is just set.

8.   Finish tart with lemon zest, more chopped chives, and shaved parmesan.

Nutrition:

- Calories: 50

- Carbs: 4g

- Fiber: 2g

- Fat: 2.5g

- Protein: 2g

Spaghetti Squash with Brown Butter and Parmesan

Preparation Time: 15 minutes

Cooking Time: 50 to 60 minutes

Servings: 5

Ingredients:

- 1 spaghetti squash, 2 ½ to 3 lb.

- 4 tbs. (½ stick) unsalted butter

- Pinch freshly grated nutmeg

- 1/3 cup grated Parmigiano-Reggiano cheese

- Salt and freshly ground pepper, to taste

Directions:

1. Place the whole squash in a large pot and add water to cover. Bring to a boil over high heat, reduce the heat to medium-low, and simmer, uncovered, until the squash can be easily pierced with a knife, about 45 minutes.

2. Meanwhile, in a saucepan over medium-high heat, melt the butter and cook it until it turns brown and just begins to smoke, 3 to 4 minutes. Remove immediately from the heat and stir in the nutmeg.

3.   When the squash is done, drain and set aside until cool enough to handle. Cut the squash in half lengthwise and, using a fork, scrape out the seeds and discard. Place the squash halves, cut sides up, on a serving platter. Using the fork, scrape the flesh free of the skin, carefully separating it into the spaghetti-like strands that it naturally forms. Leave the strands mounded in the squash halves. If the butter has cooled, place over medium heat until hot.

4.   To serve, drizzle the butter evenly over the squash. Sprinkle with the cheese and season with salt and pepper. Serve immediately.

Nutrition:

- Calories: 214.3

- Fat: 3.4g

- Saturated Fat: 1.7g

Smoked Jalapeno Poppers

Preparation Time: 10 minutes

Cooking Time: 20 to 25 minutes

Servings: 4

Ingredients:

- 12 jalapeño peppers
- 8-ounces cream cheese, room temperature
- 10 pieces bacon

Directions:

1. Preheat your grill or another wood-Traeger grill to 350°.

2. Wash and cut the tops off of the peppers, and then slice them in half the long way. Scrape the seeds and the membranes out, and set them aside.

3. Spoon softened cream cheese into the popper, and wrap with bacon and secure with a toothpick.

4. Place on wire racks that are non-stick or have been sprayed with non-stick spray, and grill for 20-25 minutes, or until the bacon is cooked.

Nutrition:

- Calories: 94

- Carbs: 5g

- Fat: 7g

Smoked Pickled Green Beans

Preparation Time: 5 minutes Cooking Time: 15 to 20 minutes

Servings: 2 Ingredients:

• 1 Lb. Green Beans, Blanched

• ½ cup Salt

• ½ cup Sugar

• 1 tbsp. Red Pepper Flake

• 2 cups White Wine Vinegar

• 2 cups Ice Water

Directions:

1. When ready to cook, set temperature to 180°F and preheat, lid closed for 15 minutes.

2. Place the blanched green beans on a mesh grill mat and place the mat directly on the grill grate. Smoke the green beans for 30-45 minutes until they've picked up the desired amount of smoke. Remove from grill and set aside until the brine is ready.

3. In a medium-sized saucepan, bring all remaining ingredients except ice water, to a boil over medium-high heat

on the stove. Simmer for 5-10 minutes then remove from heat and steep 20 minutes more. Pour brine over ice water to cool.

4.	Once the brine has cooled, pour over the green beans and weigh them down with a few plates to ensure they are completely submerged. Let sit 24 hours before use.

Nutrition: Calories: 99 Fat: 5g Carbs: 19mg

Fish & Seafood Recipes

Spiced Salmon Kebabs

Preparation Time: 20 minutes

Cooking Time: 25 minutes

Servings: 4

Ingredients:

- 2 tbsp. chopped fresh oregano

- 2 tsp. sesame seeds

- 1 tsp. ground cumin

- 1 tsp. Kosher salt

- ¼ tsp. crushed red pepper flakes

- 1 ½ pound skinless salmon fillets, cut into 1" pieces

- 2 lemons, thinly sliced into rounds

- 2 tbsp. olive oil

- 16 bamboo skewers soaked in water for one hour

Intolerances:

- Gluten-Free

- Egg-Free

- Lactose-Free

Directions:

1.   Set up the grill for medium heat. Mix the oregano, sesame seeds, cumin, salt, and red pepper flakes in a little bowl. Put the spice blend aside.

2.   String the salmon and the lemon slices onto 8 sets of parallel skewers in order to make 8 kebabs.

3.   Spoon with oil and season with the spice blend.

4.   Grill and turn at times until the fish is cooked.

Nutrition:

• Calories: 230

• Fat: 10g

• Carbs: 1g

• Protein: 30g

Buttered Clams

Preparation Time: 15 minutes

Cooking Time: 8 minutes

Servings: 6

Ingredients:

- 24 littleneck clams

- ½ cup cold butter, chopped

- 2 tbsp. fresh parsley, minced

- 3 garlic cloves, minced

- 1 tsp. fresh lemon juice

Directions:

1. Preheat the Z Grills Traeger Grill & Smoker on grill setting to 450°F.

2. Scrub the clams under cold running water.

3. In a large casserole dish, mix together the remaining ingredients.

4. Place the casserole dish onto the grill.

5. Now, arrange the clams directly onto the grill and cook for about 5-8 minutes or until they are opened. (Discard any that fail to open). With tongs, carefully transfer the opened

clams into the casserole dish and remove them from the grill.

Serve immediately.

Nutrition: Calories: 306 Fat: 17.6 g Saturated Fat: 9.9 g

Cholesterol: 118 mg Sodium: 237 mg Carbs: 6.4 g Fiber: 0.1 g

Sugar 0.1 g Protein: 29.3 g

Fish Stew

Preparation Time: 20 minutes

Cooking Time: 25 minutes

Servings: 8

Ingredients:

- 1 jar (28oz.) Crushed Tomatoes

- 2 oz. Tomato paste

- ¼ cup White wine

- ¼ cup Chicken Stock

- 2 tbsp. Butter

- 2 Garlic cloves, minced

- ¼ Onion, diced

- ½ lb. Shrimp divined and cleaned

- ½ lb. Clams

- ½ lb. Halibut

- Parsley

- Bread

Directions:

1. Preheat the grill to 300°F with a closed lid.

2.   Place a Dutch oven over medium heat and melt the butter.

3.   Sauté the onion for 4 - 7 minutes. Add the garlic. Cook for 1 more minute.

4.   Add the tomato paste. Cook until the color becomes rust red. Pour the stock and wine. Cook 10 minutes. Add the tomatoes, simmer.

5.   Chop the halibut and together with the other seafood add in the Dutch oven. Place it on the grill and cover with a lid.

6.   Let it cook for 20 minutes.

7.   Season with black pepper and salt and set aside.

8.   Top with chopped parsley and serve with bread.

9.   Enjoy!

Nutrition:

- Calories: 188

- Protein: 25g

- Carbs: 7g

- Fat: 12g

Grilled Onion Butter Cod

Preparation Time: 10 minutes

Cooking Time: 15 minutes

Servings: 4

Ingredients:

- ¼ cup butter

- 1 finely chopped small onion

- ¼ cup white wine

- 4 (6ounce) cod fillets

- 1 tbsp. extra virgin olive oil

- ½ tsp. salt (or to taste)

- ½ tsp. black pepper

- Lemon wedges

Intolerances:

- Gluten-Free

- Egg-Free

Directions:

- Set up the grill for medium-high heat.

- In a little skillet liquefy the butter. Add the onion and cook for 1or 2 minutes.

- Add the white wine and let stew for an extra 3 minutes. Take away and let it cool for 5 minutes.

- Spoon the fillets with extra virgin olive oil and sprinkle with salt and pepper. Put the fish on a well-oiled rack and cook for 8 minutes.

- Season it with sauce and cautiously flip it over. Cook for 6 to 7 minutes more, turning more times or until the fish arrives at an inside temperature of 145°F.

- Take away from the grill, top with lemon wedges, and serve.

Nutrition:

- Calories: 140

- Fat: 5g

- Cholesterol: 46mg

- Carbs: 4g

- Protein: 20g

Lemony Lobster Tails

Preparation Time: 15 minutes

Cooking Time: 25 hours Servings: 4

Ingredients:

- ½ cup butter, melted

- 2 garlic cloves, minced

- 2 tsp. fresh lemon juice

- Salt and ground black pepper, as required

- 4 (8-ounce) lobster tails

Directions:

1. Preheat the Z Grills Traeger Grill & Smoker on grill setting to 450°F.

2. In a metal pan, add all ingredients except for lobster tails and mix well.

3. Place the pan onto the grill and cook for about 10 minutes.

4. Meanwhile, cut down the top of the shell and expose lobster meat.

5. Remove pan of butter mixture from the grill.

6. Coat the lobster meat with butter mixture.

7. Place the lobster tails onto the grill and cook for about 15 minutes, coating with butter mixture once halfway through.

8. Remove from the grill and serve hot.

Nutrition: Calories: 409 Fat: 24.9 g Saturated Fat: 15.1 g Cholesterol: 392 mg Sodium: 1305 mg Carbs: 0.6 g Fiber: 0 g Sugar 0.1 g Protein: 43.5 g

Stuffed Squid on Traeger Grill

Preparation Time: 15 minutes

Cooking Time: 30 minutes

Servings: 8

Ingredients:

- 2 lbs. squid

- 4 cloves garlic

- 10 sprigs parsley

- 4 slices old bread

- 1/3 cup milk

- Salt and ground white pepper

- 4 slices prosciutto

- 4 slices cheese

- 3 tbsp. olive oil

- 1 lemon

Directions:

1. Wash and clean your squid and pat dry on a paper towel. Finely chop parsley and garlic.

2. Cut bread into cubes and soak it in milk.

3.   Add parsley, garlic, white pepper, and salt. Stir well together.

4.   Cut the cheese into larger pieces (the pieces should be large enough that they can be pushed through the opening of the squid).

5.   Mix the cheese with prosciutto slices and stir well together with the remaining ingredients.

6.   Use your fingers to open the bag pack of squid and pushed the mixture inside. At the end add some more bread.

7.   Close the openings with toothpicks.

8.   Start your Traeger grill on smoke with the lid open for 5 minutes.

9.   Set the temperature to the highest setting and preheat, lid closed, for 10 – 15 minutes.

10.   Grill squid for 3 – 4 minutes being careful not to burn the squid. Serve hot.

Nutrition:

- Calories: 290

- Fat: 13g

- Cholesterol: 288mg

- Carbs: 13g

- Protein: 25g

Cheese and Breads

Grilled Homemade Croutons

Preparation Time: 10 minutes

Cooking Time: 30 minutes

Servings: 6

Ingredients:

- 2 tbsp. Mediterranean Blend Seasoning

- ¼ cup olive oil

- 6 cups cubed bread

Directions:

1. Preheat your Traeger grill to 250°F.

2. Combine seasoning and oil in a bowl then drizzle the mixture over the bread cubes. Toss to evenly coat.

3. Layer the bread cubes on a cookie sheet, large, and place them on the grill.

4. Bake for about 30 minutes. Stir at intervals of 5 minutes for browning evenly.

5.   Once dried out and golden brown, remove from the grill.

6.   Serve and enjoy!

Nutrition:

•   Calories: 188 Fat: 10g

•   Saturated Fat: 2gCarbs: 20g

•   Net Carbs: 19g Protein: 4g

•   Sugars: 2g Fiber: 1g

•   Sodium: 1716mg Potassium: 875mg

Rub and Sauces Recipes

Smoked Cherry BBQ Sauce

Preparation Time: 20 minutes

Cooking Time: 1 hour

Servings: 2

Ingredients:

- 2 lb. dark sweet cherries, pitted

- 1 large chopped onion

- ½ tbsp. red pepper flakes, crushed

- 1 tbsp. kosher salt or to taste

- ½ tbsp. ginger, ground

- ½ tbsp. black pepper

- ½ tbsp. cumin

- ½ tbsp. cayenne pepper

- 1 tbsp. onion powder

- 1 tbsp. garlic powder

- 1 tbsp. smoked paprika

- 2 chopped garlic cloves

- ½ cup pinot noir

- 2 tbsp. yellow mustard

- 1-½ cups ketchup

- 2 tbsp. balsamic vinegar

- 1/3 cup apple cider vinegar

- 2 tbsp. dark soy sauce

- 1 tbsp. liquid smoke

- ¼ cup Worcestershire sauce

- 1 tbsp. hatch Chile powder

- 3 tbsp. honey

- 1 cup brown sugar

- 3 tbsp. molasses

Directions:

1. Preheat your smoker to 250°F.

2. Place cherries in a baking dish, medium, and smoke for about 2 hours.

3. Sauté onions and red pepper flakes in a pot, large, with 2 tbsp. oil for about 4 minutes until softened.

4. Add salt and cook for an additional 1 minute.

5. Add ginger, black pepper, cumin, onion powder, garlic powder, and paprika then drizzle with oil and cook for about 1 minute until fragrant and spices bloom.

6. Stir in garlic and cook for about 30 seconds.

7.   Pour in pinot noir scraping up for 1 minute for any bits stuck to your pan bottom.

8.   Add yellow mustard, ketchup, balsamic vinegar, apple cider vinegar, dark soy sauce, liquid smoke, and Worcestershire sauce. Stir to combine.

9.   Add cherries and simmer for about 10 minutes.

10.   Add honey, brown sugar, and molasses, and stir until combined. Simmer for about 30-45 minutes over low heat until your liking. Place everything into a blender and process until a smooth sauce. Enjoy with favorite veggies or protein. You can refrigerate in jars for up to a month.

Nutrition: Calories: 35   Fat: 0g Carbs: 9g Protein: 0g Fiber: 0g

Nut, Fruits and Dessert

Apple Cobbler

Preparation Time: 30 minutes

Cooking Time: 1 hour and 50 minutes

Servings: 8

Ingredients:

- 8 Granny Smith apples

- 1 cup sugar

- 1 stick melted butter

- 1 tsp. cinnamon

- Pinch salt

- ½ cup brown sugar

- 2 eggs

- 2 tsp. baking powder

- 2 cups plain flour

- 1 ½ cup sugar

Directions:

1. Peel and quarter apples, place into a bowl. Add in the cinnamon and one c. sugar. Stir well to coat and let it sit for one hour.

2.   Add Traegers to your smoker and follow your cooker's startup procedure. Preheat your smoker, with your lid closed, until it reaches 350.

3.   In a large bowl add the salt, baking powder, eggs, brown sugar, sugar, and flour. Mix until it forms crumbles.

4.   Place apples into a Dutch oven. Add the crumble mixture on top and drizzle with melted butter.

5.   Place on the grill and cook for 50 minutes.

Nutrition:

- Calories: 216.7

- Protein: 2.7g

- Fiber: 0g

- Carbs: 41g

Fat: 4.7g

Chocolate Chip Cookies

Preparation Time: 30 minutes

Cooking Time: 30 minutes

Servings: 1

Ingredients:

- 1 ½ cup chopped walnuts

- 1 tsp. vanilla

- 2 cup chocolate chips

- 1 tsp. baking soda

- 2 ½ cups plain flour

- ½ tsp. salt

- 1 ½ stick softened butter

- 2 eggs

- 1 cup brown sugar

- ½ cup sugar

Directions:

1.   Add Traegers to your smoker and follow your cooker's startup procedure. Preheat your smoker, with your lid closed, until it reaches 350°F.

2.   Mix together the baking soda, salt, and flour.

3.   Cream the brown sugar, sugar, and butter. Mix in the vanilla and eggs until it comes together.

4.   Slowly add in the flour while continuing to beat. Once all flour has been incorporated, add in the chocolate chips and walnuts. Using a spoon, fold into batter.

5.   Place an aluminum foil onto the grill. In an aluminum foil, drop spoonfuls of dough and bake for 17 minutes.

Nutrition:

- Calories: 66.5

- Protein: 1.8g

- Fiber: 0g

- Carbs: 5.9g

- Fat: 4.6g

Lamb Recipes

Lamb Chops

Preparation Time: 10 minutes

Cooking Time: 10 minutes

Servings: 8

Ingredients:

For the Lamb:

- 16 lamb chops, fat trimmed

- 2 tbsp. Greek Freak seasoning

For the Mint Sauce:

- 1 tbsp. chopped parsley

- 12 cloves garlic, peeled

- 1 tbsp. chopped mint

- ¼ tsp. dried oregano

- 1 tsp. salt

- ¼ tsp. ground black pepper

- ¾ cup lemon juice

- 1 cup olive oil

Directions:

1. Prepare the mint sauce and for this, place all of its ingredients in a food processor and then pulse for 1 minute until smooth.

2. Pour 1/3 cup of the mint sauce into a plastic bag, add lamb chops in it, seal the bag, turn it upside to coat lamb chops with the sauce and then let them marinate for a minimum of 30 minutes in the refrigerator.

3. When ready to cook, switch on the Traeger grill, fill the grill hopper with apple-flavored Traegers, power the grill on by using the control panel, select 'smoke' on the temperature dial, or set the temperature to 450°F and let it preheat for a minimum of 15 minutes.

4. Meanwhile, remove lamb chops from the marinade and then season with Greek seasoning.

5. When the grill has preheated, open the lid, place lamb chops on the grill grate, shut the grill, and smoke for 4 to 5 minutes per side until cooked to the desired level.

6. When done, transfer the lamb chops to a dish and then serves.

Nutrition:

- Calories: 362

- Fat: 26 g

- Carbs: 0 g

- Protein: 31 g

- Fiber: 0 g

Greek-Style Roast Leg of Lamb

Preparation Time: 25 minutes

Cooking Time: 1 hour and 30 minutes

Servings: 12

Ingredients:

- 7 pounds leg lamb, bone-in, fat trimmed

- 2 lemons, juiced

- 8 cloves garlic, peeled, minced

- Salt as needed

- Ground black pepper as needed

- 1 tsp. dried oregano

- 1 tsp. dried rosemary

- 6 tbsp. olive oil

Directions:

1. Make a small cut into the meat of lamb by using a paring knife, then stir together garlic, oregano, and rosemary and stuff this paste into the slits of the lamb meat.

2. Take a roasting pan, place lamb in it, then rub with lemon juice and olive oil, cover with a plastic wrap and let marinate for a minimum of 8 hours in the refrigerator.

3.   When ready to cook, switch on the Traeger grill, fill the grill hopper with oak flavored Traegers, power the grill on by using the control panel, select 'smoke' on the temperature dial, or set the temperature to 400°F and let it preheat for a minimum of 15 minutes.

4.   Meanwhile, remove the lamb from the refrigerator, bring it to room temperature, uncover it and then season well with salt and black pepper.

5.   When the grill has preheated, open the lid, place food on the grill grate, shut the grill, and smoke for 30 minutes.

6.   Change the smoking temperature to 350°F and then continue smoking for 1 hour until the internal temperature reaches 140°F.

7.   When done, transfer lamb to a cutting board, let it rest for 15 minutes, then cut it into slices and serve.

Nutrition:

- Calories: 168

- Fat: 10 g

- Carbs: 2 g

- Protein: 17 g

- Fiber: 0.7 g

Rosemary-Smoked Lamb Chops

Preparation Time: 15 minutes

Cooking Time: 2 hours and 5 minutes

Servings: 4

Ingredients:

- Traeger Flavor: Mesquite

- 4½ pounds bone-in lamb chops

- 2 tbsp. olive oil

- Salt

- Freshly ground black pepper

- 1 bunch fresh rosemary

Directions:

1. Supply your smoker with Traeger and follow the manufacturer's specific start-up procedure. Preheat the grill to 180°F.

2. Rub the lamb generously with olive oil and season on both sides with salt and pepper.

3. Spread the rosemary directly on the grill grate, creating a surface area large enough for all the chops to rest on. Place the chops on the rosemary and smoke until they reach an internal temperature of 135°F.

4. Increase the grill's temperature to 450°F, remove the rosemary, and continue to cook the chops until their internal temperature reaches 145°F.

5. Take off the chops from the grill and let them rest for 5 minutes before serving.

Nutrition:

- Calories: 50

- Carbs: 4g

- Fiber: 2g

- Fat: 2.5g

- Protein: 2g

Appetizers and Sides

Spinach Salad with Avocado and Orange

Preparation Time: 5 Minutes

Cooking Time: 20 Minutes

Servings: 4

Ingredients:

- 1 ½ tbsp. fresh lime juice
- 4 tsp. extra-virgin olive oil
- 1 tbsp. chopped fresh cilantro
- 1/8 tsp. kosher salt
- ½ cup diced peeled ripe avocado
- ½ cup fresh orange segments
- 1 (5-ounce) package baby spinach
- 1/8 tsp. freshly ground black pepper

Directions:

1. Combine the first 4 substances in a bowl, stirring with a whisk.

2. Combine avocado, orange segments, and spinach in a bowl. Add oil combination; toss. Sprinkle salad with black pepper.

Nutrition:

- Calories: 103

- Fat: 7.3g

- Sodium: 118mg

Fresh Creamed Corn

Preparation Time: 5 Minutes

Cooking Time: 30 Minutes

Servings: 4

Ingredients:

- 2 tsp. unsalted butter

- 2 cups fresh corn kernels

- 2 tbsp. minced shallots

- ¾ cup 1% low-fat milk

- 2 tsp. all-purpose flour

- ¼ tsp. salt

Directions:

1. Melt butter in a huge nonstick skillet over medium-excessive warmness.

2. Add corn and minced shallots to pan; prepare dinner for 1 minute, stirring constantly.

3. Add milk, flour, and salt to pan; bring to a boil.

4. Reduce warmness to low; cover and cook dinner for 4 minutes.

Nutrition:

- Calories: 107

- Fat: 3.4g

- Protein: 4g

- Carb: 18g

Watermelon-Cucumber Salad

Preparation Time: 12 Minutes

Cooking Time: 0 Minutes

Servings: 4

Ingredients:

- 1 tbsp. olive oil

- 2 tsp. fresh lemon juice

- ¼ tsp. salt

- 2 cups cubed seedless watermelon

- 1 cup thinly sliced English cucumber

- ¼ cup thinly vertically sliced red onion

- 1 tbsp. thinly sliced fresh basil

Directions:

1. Consolidate oil, squeeze, and salt in a huge bowl, mixing great.

2. Include watermelon, cucumber, and onion; toss well to coat. Sprinkle plate of mixed greens equally with basil.

Nutrition:

- Calories: 60

- Fat: 3.5g

- Protein: 0.8g

- Carb 7.6g

Traditional Recipes

Chicken Casserole

Preparation Time: 15 minutes

Cooking Time: 55 minutes

Servings: 8

Ingredients:

- 2 (15-ounce) cans cream of chicken soup

- 2 cups milk

- 2 tbsp. unsalted butter

- ¼ cup all-purpose flour

- 1 pound skinless, boneless chicken thighs, chopped

- ½ cup hatch chiles, chopped

- 2 medium onions, chopped

- 1 tbsp. fresh thyme, chopped

- Salt and ground black pepper, as required

- 1 cup cooked bacon, chopped

- 1 cup tater tots

Directions:

1. Preheat the Traeger grill & Smoker on grill setting to 400°F.

2. In a large bowl, mix together chicken soup and milk.

3. In a skillet, melt butter over medium heat.

4. Slowly, add flour and cook for about 1-2 minutes or until smooth, stirring continuously.

5. Slowly, add soup mixture, beating continuously until smooth.

6. Cook until the mixture starts to thicken, stirring continuously.

7. Stir in remaining ingredients except for bacon and simmer for about 10-15 minutes.

8. Stir in bacon and transfer mixture into a 2½-quart casserole dish.

9. Place tater tots on top of the casserole evenly.

10. Arrange the pan onto the grill and cook for about 30-35 minutes.

11. Serve hot.

Nutrition:

Calories: 440 Fat: 25.8 g

Saturated Fat: 9.3 g Cholesterol: 86 mg

Sodium: 1565 mg

Carbs: 22.2 g

Fiber: 1.5 g

Sugar: 4.6 g

Protein: 28.9 g

Glazed Chicken Wings

Preparation Time: 15 minutes

Cooking Time: 2 hours

Servings: 6

Ingredients:

- 2 pounds' chicken wings

- 2 garlic cloves, crushed

- 3 tbsp. hoisin sauce

- 2 tbsp. soy sauce

- 1 tsp. dark sesame oil

- 1 tbsp. honey

- ½ tsp. ginger powder

- 1 tbsp. sesame seeds, toasted lightly

Directions:

1. Preheat the Traeger grill & Smoker on grill setting to 225°F.

2. Arrange the wings onto the lower rack of the grill and cook for about 1½ hours.

3. Meanwhile, in a large bowl, mix together remaining all ingredients.

4. Remove wings from grill and place in the bowl of garlic mixture.

5. Coat wings with garlic mixture generously.

6. Now, set the grill to 375°F.

7. Arrange the coated wings onto a foil-lined baking sheet and sprinkle with sesame seeds.

8. Place the pan onto the lower rack of the traeger grill and cook for about 25-30 minutes.

9. Serve immediately.

Nutrition:

Calories: 336

Fat: 13 g

Saturated Fat: 3.3 g

Cholesterol: 135 mg

Sodium: 560 mg

Carbs: 7.6 g

Fiber: 0.5 g

Sugar: 5.2 g

Protein: 44.7 g

CPSIA information can be obtained
at www.ICGtesting.com
Printed in the USA
BVHW090132240521
607980BV00007B/125